Glorious LINENS

MAY GOD BLESS YOU

Martha Pullen

The Martha Pullen Company

Publisher:
Martha Pullen
The Martha Pullen Company
149 Old Big Cove Road
Brownsboro, Alabama 35741
www.marthapullen.com

Editor: Elizabeth Pugh
Written by Elizabeth Pugh
Embroidery Design by Angela Pullen Atherton

Hoffman Media, LLC.

President:
Phyllis Hoffman
Hoffman Media, LLC.
1900 International Park Drive, Suite 50
Birmingham, Alabama 35243

Production Direction by Greg Baugh
Graphic Design by Jordan Marxer
Photography by Marcy Black
Contributing Photography by Mac Jamieson
Styling by Molly Smith
Color Correction by Delisa McDaniel
Copy Editing by Wanda Billings and Karen Dauphin

Printed in the United States of America

ISBN# 0978548981

Glorious LINENS

A Publication of Martha Pullen Co., Inc.

CONTENTS

INTRODUCTION

Every piece of linen tells a story...

The linens in this book tell the story of another time. They tell the story of a time when linen treasures were made by hand at home and not bought in a store; when every observer knew with a glance the hours, skill, and care that went into the linen's careful construction; when linens, prized equally by men and women, were passed down from generation to generation as items of importance; when the ubiquitous presence of linens signaled their owners' refinement and taste; when linens were a cultural currency valued by those who had them, appreciated by those who didn't, and longed for by all.

If the linens of this book had a human voice, they would mesmerize us with their tales that span decades and centuries: tales of weddings and births, of grand banquets and simple meals, of quiet domesticity in the midst of a changing world. Silent sentries standing watch over the passing of generations, these marvelous linens were faithful servants called into duty by owners whose names we do not know—called to cushion a sleeping head, to wipe crumbs from a mouth, to shield a table from the hard dinnerware, to bring a touch of gaiety to a solemn room.

For those of us who care to listen, however, these linens speak to both our hearts and our heads. One cannot look at the impossibly intricate needle lace of an eighteenth-century banquet-sized tablecloth and not feel the soul of its anonymous maker emanating from every perfectly crafted loop, stitch, and knot. Nor can one look at the frayed edging of a child's lace pillow and not feel how intensely this object was loved by a child, loved so intensely that the pillow remains long after the child is gone. And one cannot look at the twining monogram of a trousseau set—sheets, pillows, napkins, and tablecloths—and not imagine the feelings of duty, wonder, and anticipation that a young girl felt as she crafted the items that she would take into her new life as wife and mother. These are the kinds of stories that these linens have to tell.

This book is for those who look at the handwork from centuries past with a sense of awe, wonder, and inquisitiveness. It is for those who long to hold crisp antique linen in their hands and to imagine the hands that crafted it and the home that first housed it. It is for those who see a rich life story shining from within the most timeworn of linens and cherish it for its enduring beauty. We hope these images inspire you to cultivate the beauty within your own home, so that the treasured keepsakes of your own life will leave an indelible imprint for the generations to come.

Linens
TELL A STORY OF
Artistry & Craftmanship

For centuries, it was an early rite of passage: a young girl would sit next to her mother's side, fabric and needle in hand, and learn to make tiny stitches upon a simple practice cloth. As her stitches became more even and precise, when the back of her work was as tidy as the front, then would the young student begin her duties in earnest: embroidering clothing and household linens. At its most basic, the need for embroidery upon linens was a utilitarian task; they needed to be marked for ownership. At its most breathtaking, however, embroidery upon linens became an outlet for artistic expression, one in which the skilled needleworker could create landscapes, portraits, and tableaux whose beauty rivaled the finest paintings of the day. In a time when most women could not read or write, when equipped with needle and thread they could still express themselves artistically.

The basic repertoire of stitches upon fabric can be broken down into a few general categories: cross, satin, and straight stitches; looped and knotted stitches; and, adding a bit more complexity, pulled-thread, withdrawn-thread, cutwork, and needle-lace techniques. Working within these broad categories, needleworkers of

THIS PAGE: Placemat with chemical-lace edging, early twentieth century. "Chemical lace" refers to a technique in which intricate patterns were machine embroidered on a dissolvable background fabric. They typically appear as edgings on small items.

the past could create an infinite number of effects, ranging from simple to sublime.

Anyone who has attempted the more advanced handwork techniques of the past has been awed by what our forbearers accomplished without the aid of electric lighting or magnifying glasses. With nimble, agile fingers, they knew by touch and intuition when their stitches had perfect tension, perfect spacing, and a perfect twist to their floss; they could feel the gentle friction as fibers and filaments slid across one another before locking into place with the gentlest of tugs. Not by eyesight alone were the fabric-and-thread masterpieces of the past created, but through keen perception and gentle wisdom that rivals that possessed by any architect, artist, or engineer of our modern age.

A constellation of tiny stitches creates fanciful images from thin air.

THIS PAGE: Needlelace tablecloth with figurals, Italian, mid
nineteenth century. OPPOSITE
PAGE, BOTTOM: Detail of
needlelace tablecloth. OPPO-
SITE PAGE, TOP: Tablecloth
with drawn-thread work, satin
stitch, and eyelet stitches.

The endurance of antique and vintage linens is a *testament to the skill* with which they were made.

TOP: Details of tablecloth needlelace insertions. Italian, late nineteenth century. RIGHT: Detail of cutwork linen bed cover, Austro-Hungarian Empire period. This figural panel is located in the center of the bed cover. OPPOSITE PAGE: Handkerchief with bobbinlace edging, early twentieth century.

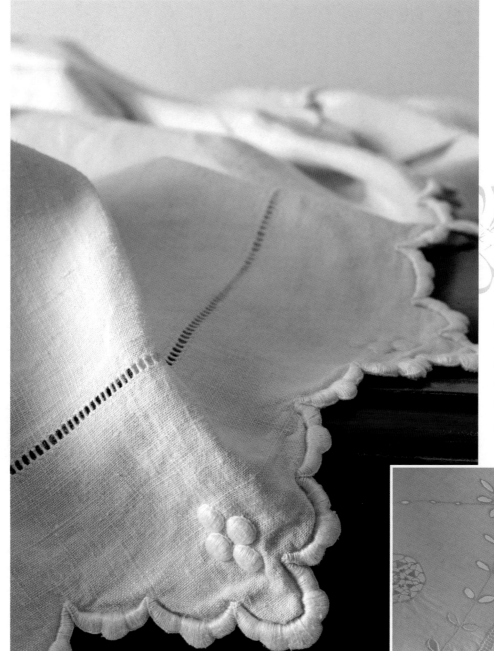

LEFT: Vintage linen bed sheet with drawn-thread border and scalloped and padded satin-stitch edging. BELOW: Round eyelet tablecloth with filet lace and needlelace insertions, early twentieth century. OPPOSITE PAGE: Ecru linen napkins with handmade needlelace edging.

The texture of *densely worked stitches* beckons you to come forward and touch them

phyllis hoffman
• A COLLECTOR'S PORTRAIT •

Ask Phyllis Hoffman what type of embroidered linen is her favorite and her eyes narrow to slits and take on a faraway look as she searches through her mental inventory. "I can't choose," she says decisively after only five or ten seconds, "I love them all." The resolute tone of her voice is that of a proud mother, fending off requests to name a favorite from among her own children. It can't be done.

When discussing antique linens with Phyllis, one might anticipate to encounter Phyllis Hoffman the businesswoman—an entrepreneur who founded the country's first cross-stitch magazine and another devoted specifically to antique needlework; a business woman who parlayed two small magazines about embroidery into a multifaceted company that publishes numerous titles embracing a range of lifestyle topics; an astute linen collector who knows the nuances of technique that determine a piece's worth and who has the trained eye to spot a bargain or a once-in-a-lifetime rarity.

But when discussing antique linens with Phyllis Hoffman, it quickly becomes apparent that one is dealing with Phyllis the needlework enthusiast—the hand-sewing purist who learned her skills as a child at her mother and grandmother's sides; the needlework evangelist who, as a young accountant beginning her career, carried an audit bag in one hand and a needlework bag in the other during her days on the road; the creative spirit who somehow finds time to create counted-thread designs for a loyal

OPPOSITE PAGE: Chemical-lace placemat with figurals, early twentieth century. THIS PAGE: Linen napkin with padded satin-stitch monogram, cutwork, and filet-lace edging.

audience inspired by the skilled needlewomen of centuries past. For Phyllis, antique linens are first and foremost a passion, not a simple hobby or a business investment. It's in her blood.

"In my family, the textiles of the home were made by the women of the family," Phyllis says. They lavished attention upon utilitarian items that served as the family's faithful servants through both waking and sleeping hours—pillow shams, sheets, and tablecloths—bringing artistry to the commonplace and familiar. Although Phyllis became a connoisseur of antique linens as an adult, the appreciation she developed for handwork as a child keeps this appreciation rooted firmly in the process of handwork. While she can't decide upon a favorite style of embroidery, she can pick—when absolutely forced to by a persistent interviewer—which item from her linen collection she would save if she could only save one thing: a collection of doilies hand crocheted by the women in her family, which are framed and hanging in her sewing room. "I have more valuable pieces. But knowing they were worked by the women in my family, knowing where they came from…that's where the greatest value is for me."

"What I love about handwork is that it's something that doesn't come undone. We live in a disposable culture, but this is a work of art that can be whatever you choose. It's lasting."

A passion for handwork is encoded in Phyllis' DNA. She has allowed herself to change the application of her needlework to suit the times, but she has never for a moment put her needles away. When she wished for but couldn't find a magazine devoted to counted cross-stitch in the 1980s, she founded her own. At that moment needlework crossed over from her personal life to her professional life and, as the publisher of a magazine devoted to antique needlework, she obtained a rarified education that would turn most needlework collectors green with envy. "It's really just about loving linen. I can appreciate the time that went into them," says Phyllis.

This collector of handwork, however, will never cease to be a creator of handwork. "What I love about handwork is that it's something that doesn't come undone. We live in a disposable culture, but this is a work of art that can be whatever you choose. It's lasting," Phyllis says. "Plus there's the thrill out of saying, 'I did it myself.'" To be sure, she's a handwork purist, but she's not opposed to calling her sewing machine into service. "There are such wonderful machines available today. It takes a long time to produce an elaborate piece of handwork, but machines can make exquisite patterns quickly," she adds.

Phyllis often calls upon her sewing machine for its monogramming capability. Monograms are a particular passion of Phyllis' that embraces both the old and the new. "I've always been intrigued by monograms—particularly those that intertwine. The engineering is fascinating," Phyllis says. All of her guest linens are monogrammed, and she always has her eyes peeled for exquisite monograms when antique shopping. ("It's electric when you find your own monogram!") She's not averse to buying monogrammed pieces that don't match her own initials: "It's perfectly fine to enjoy something just because of the workmanship.

RIGHT: A variety of lace edgings, including (in foreground) an antimacassar with machine netting and chemical-lace edging. OPPOSITE PAGE: Figural detail of punchwork-style tablecloth, late nineteenth century. Punchwork is a form of drawnwork that resembles filet lace with its grid-like patterns.

It needs a home and someone to take care of it."

Despite the trajectory of her professional career, Phyllis' attitude toward antique and vintage linens has never changed: she still wants to live surrounded by them and she wants to be able to touch them. "I like things that I can use. I'm not into buying things that I'm going to stick in a drawer," she says. She keeps her linens out; she rotates them and handles them. "When it comes to decorating with a piece of linen, you must treat it like a work of art. Even in a minimalist home, embroidery can be used in a contemporary decorating scheme. Simple lines are beautiful. Even just simple hemstitching on a plain linen tablecloth creates a tailored look that has a more elegant appearance."

It was upon the love of stitching that Phyllis founded Hoffman Media and it was upon the love of home that she expanded her company and made it flourish. The two concepts are inextricably intertwined. "Hoffman Media produces products for women who want to put a personal touch on their lives," she says. She sees a disconnect between the idea of a career woman and the idea of a homemaker because "we all want to touch beautiful things"; her publications bridge this gap. The success in her business aside, she's happy about her role in helping women add beauty to their environments—which she realizes is quite the time-honored tradition: "It is just a thrill to see growth because of women celebrating being women!" ▨

Crisp linen and sheer organdy
combine in a union that is a feast *for the fingertips.*

PREVIOUS PAGE: Napkins and placemat with organdy corner insertions and appliqué flowers and leaves, early twentieth century. LEFT: Detail of linen tablecloth with bobbin-lace insertion, early twentieth century. BELOW: Transylvanian hand-loomed, white-on-white striped cotton joined with tape lace insertions and finished with eyelet design at top and bottom.

Using a needle as a paintbrush, the skilled embroideress makes stitches bloom on her delicate canvas of sheer cotton voile.

Centerpieces
AND DOILIES

DESCRIBED BY CHRISTINE FERRY

In no way, perhaps, is the individuality of the home maker more strongly expressed than in the decorative pieces of linen used on dining and living room tables. Embroideries, handsome enough in themselves are decidedly out of place unless they harmonize in both color and design with the other furnishing of the room and the general style of decoration, and this should always be considered.

For general purposes there is nothing quite so satisfactory as ecru or gray linen for table centrepieces, for it forms an excellent background for any color scheme, and does not show dust so quickly as does white linen. There are so many places in the home where an embroidered table piece is desirable, that one can hardly have too many. It has become quite the custom to use large, handsomely embroidered centerpieces on the dining room table between meals, and there is always a place for them in the library or living room. In the sleeping room, too, a small round table is always desirable, and it is here that white linen pieces, embroidered in color, may be used in good taste.

Lace makes a pretty finish for the edges of large centerpieces, and may be used instead of buttonholed scallops if preferred. Either effect is good.

—*The Modern Priscilla*
December 1911

OPPOSITE: Tablecloth with cutwork and Milanese lace insertions, Italian, late-nineteenth century. Milanese lace, a bobbin lace, was a luxury attainable by only the wealthy. At its height of its popularity during the first quarter of the eighteenth century, examples of Milanese lace became less ambitious and smaller in scope when airier Belgian laces became the vogue later in the century. RIGHT: Detail of Milanese lace insertion.

· Combined LACES ·

When searching through examples of antiques textiles, combinations of various techniques are a common find. Cutwork tablecloths with filet lace borders or insertions, like those shown here, are more common than those with needle-lace or filet-lace insertions. Besides ingenuity, combinations of lace often demonstrated a practical purpose: such as reducing the time or expense required to create a larger piece of linen by substituting machine-made lace or lace panels made by more than one person.

Linens
TELL A STORY OF
Refinement

In a word, we have tried to give instructions in all things pertaining to the home beautiful...that no household, however humble, need be without the refining influence of dainty environments.

Thus writes Mrs. Addie E. Heron in the 1894 introduction to *Dainty Work for Pleasure and Profit*. In subsequent pages she instructs homemakers on practical details for executing numerous types of embroidery, laces, drawn work, crochet, and knitting. Her vocabulary, jargon, and instructional philosophy make clear that the popular audience of 1894 had a much better working knowledge of embroidery than does the niche audience for fine handwork in the early twenty-first century. These "dainty trifles" with which Mrs. Heron exhorts her pupils to beautify their homes are, for the contemporary connoisseur of linens, wonders of skill, patience, and imagination.

Just as fascinating, however, is the marvelously democratic assumption with which *Dainty Work for Pleasure and Profit* was written: that growing access to quality fabrics, flosses, and sewing notions at the close of the nineteenth century put

PREVIOUS PAGE: Organza coasters, early to mid-nineteenth century. Appenzell work and satin stitch. Figurals indicate Colonial, possibly Polynesian, influence. RIGHT: Damask napkins with knotted fringe, embroidered in cross stitch, running stitch, and "PB" monogram. Mid-nineteenth century. OPPOSITE: Cotton drawn-work tablecloth, early twentieth century. BELOW: Detail of needle weaving motif at corner of drawn-work section.

the symbols of refined taste within the grasp of anyone who studiously put needle to fabric. Long gone were the days when fine embroidery was the domain of royalty and nobility; needleworkers at the dawn of the twentieth century had both the knowledge and the tools to fashion an elegant home environment for themselves. Embroidered tea cloths, table covers, draperies, doilies, and sofa cushions: these were the accoutrements of the aspiring ladies of the manor. Even the simplest and barest of dwellings, Mrs. Heron stresses, could "be made a lovely home, if only the spirit of home beautifying abides in the heart of its mistress."

"No household, however humble, need be without the refining influence of *dainty environments."*

—*Dainty Work for Pleasure and Profit* (1896)

RIGHT: Cotton pillowcase, early twentieth century. Pillowcase at left embellished with cutwork and faded red satin-stitch embroidery (left). BC monogram indicates art-nouveau influence. Cotton damask pillowcase at right embellished with blue satin-stitch embroidery and appliquéd monogram and leaves. BELOW: This exquisite place mat and napkins—worked in pink and blue satin stitches on organdy—are an example of Marghab embroidery, often considered the "Tiffany" of linen techniques. Marghab is a close cousin of Madiera embroidery, named for the island off the coast of Portugal where the technique originated, where a tradition of fine needlework extends back for more than two centuries. Having graced the tables of twentieth-century royals, vintage Marghab linens today are highly collectible and avidly sought-after items.

Soft colors such as pink and blue stand out amongst a sea of white-on-white linens, like icing on a scrumptious vanilla cake.

LEFT: Filet lace and netting window cover, decorated with linen and metallic needleweaving, crochet tassels, padded crochet grapes, fashioned into a pair of café curtains. Early twentieth century. East-European origin. RIGHT: Rustic round table cloth on coarse linen with satin-stitch motifs in bold colors and crochet trim. BELOW: Linen coaster with simple drawn-thread work and applied bobbin-lace trim.

Whether simple or elaborate, handmade linens bring distinction to a home.

martha lauren
• A COLLECTOR'S PORTRAIT •

A few dozen paces from the junction where Canterbury Road meets Petticoat Lane in Mountain Brook, Alabama, delicate antique lace curtains hang in a small storefront window. They're parted to reveal an ever-changing display of white-on-white linens—pillows and tablecloths, handkerchiefs and napkins—gems from an era gone by that have long outlived their original owners and have made their way from near and far to this little shop nestled between antique shops and fine clothiers. The nameplate on the window reads "Martha Lauren Fine Linens and Accessories" and you can smell the scent of lavender linen water before you've even opened the door.

The interior of the store is a salve for the senses that may have become overwhelmed by the multi-tasking, cellphone-toting, web-surfing culture that is ours today. Inside the shop, the cool blue walls and a constellation of starched and pressed white linens and vintage dresses take shoppers back instantly to a time when the days passed a little slower and moments were savored a little longer; even the white ceiling fan rotating overhead seems like something out of Faulkner's Old South. Behind an antique French display case containing antique silver brush-and-mirror sets, powder jars, and rouge pots you'll find the shop's namesake, Martha Lauren. This shop is the realization of a dream she didn't know she had.

Martha comes to her appreciation of fine handwork by osmosis. Her grandmother was an accom-

Table runner, English, late nineteenth century. Cutwork with simple bars and picots; padded satin-stitch monogram. OPPOSITE: Place mat and napkin, early twentieth century. Madiera work.

plished seamstress who could look at any garment and reproduce it with splendid results, and without a pattern. Martha's mother was also a virtuoso with the needle who hand-made and hand-embellished clothes in her home in Alabama to be sold in clothing shops in New England. For Martha she made organdy dresses accented with lace. "My interest evolved from seeing the way they worked and taught me the appreciation of fine handwork at an early age." Martha herself enjoyed making samplers full of the delicate stitches her mother and grandmother taught her; although, "once I got into it I found that I didn't have time for it."

A meandering path led Martha from a childhood surrounded by fine handwork to a career trading in fine handwork. For years she performed freelance work making custom draperies for private clients—hard work that required physical stamina, an artist's eye, and a tailor's skill. At the same time she indulged her love of vintage treasures by operating a booth at a Birmingham antique mall at which she sold antique wicker, wrought iron, picture frames, and—of course—some antique linens.

The idea to open a shop devoted to handwork wasn't Martha's—it was her customers'. Over the years, the clientele for Martha's two businesses had cross-pollinated and, in the process, a bit of privileged information had escaped and was making the rounds via word of mouth: Martha had a converted mother-in-law's apartment in her home that was devoted exclusively to her collection of antique and vintage linens and clothing. Clients searching for a particular type of antique handwork would eventually find their way into Martha's private sanctuary.

Encouraged by her husband, Tom, Martha opened her shop on Canterbury Road in 2001, filling it with the treasures from her collection at home.

Standing in her shop, amidst a sea of white, Martha is the picture of a person who has found her perfect spot in life: she's quite literally surrounded by what she loves. Her favorite types of linen are Normandy lace and filet lace, although she's also drawn to curtains and has a soft spot in her heart for netted lace panels. She enjoys hearing the reactions of customers when they enter her shop for the first time and begin browsing through her wares. "For a lot of people being in my shop reminds them of things in their grandmother's home. Or they'll remember things they have at home that they need to get out of a drawer and use," Martha says. She enjoys talking with her customers, encouraging them to unearth the family treasures they have tucked away and forgotten at home. "Those linens passed down to you from your grandmother—don't pack them away. Get them out and use them. Don't be afraid to put them out."

"Those linens passed down to you from your grandmother— don't pack them away. Get them out and use them."

Martha does have a few important caveats regarding the use of vintage and antique linens, however. Most importantly, wash linens by hand, always. Rinse them in cold water, and never store them away ironed. While a variety of modern

cleaning solutions do wonders at getting out stubborn stains, Martha suggests two make-at-home solutions that work just as well. "Put lemon and salt on spots and lay the piece out on the grass in the sunshine. That will get it every time," Martha says. Another quick fix? Mix Cascade® dishwashing granules and hydrogen peroxide to form a paste and then apply to stained linens and let sit for a while.

The reverie of Martha's store is at times broken by the jangle of a cell phone ring, bringing shoppers out of their sojourn in the past and back to the present time. "It's a busy world we live in, and people enjoy the step back in time to a simple quiet atmosphere," Martha says. "I'm lucky in that I've lived in both worlds…the quiet world and today. But I enjoy both. I know how to back off and have quiet time. But I run a business, so I stay busy." For those people looking for a brief respite from modern times by surrounding themselves with heirlooms from centuries past, Martha's store is a welcome treat. She's open five days a week on Canterbury Lane, just a few dozen paces down from the junction with Petticoat Lane. ▦

ABOVE: Lampshade cover, early twentieth century. Handmade Brussels lace. Impractical as lampshade because heat from light damages lace. RIGHT: Detail of napkin, early twentieth century. Madeira work with tan satin stitches and simple bars.

Work -
FOR NIMBLE FINGERS

BY M.C. HUNGERFORD

There are fashions in fancy work, as in most other mutable things with which frail humanity has to deal. Change, which is the order of our being, governs our taste to a great extent. The coming fancy, as near as one can predict, is for some glow of color in decoration. White, which is in perfect taste, has been for some time universally liked for embellishing articles intended for table use, but now many of the most beautiful pieces are embroidered with colored silks which show perfect fidelity to the natural shades of the flowers depicted. The perfection now attained in the dyeing of silk, both as to shade and durability makes the embroiderer's art most satisfactory. There is quite a return to the fashion of fifty years ago in the supply of pure colors now shown, but there is an assertion of improved modernity in the vast number of successive shades of each pure color. With these means at hand the needleworker's experiments become easier and far more artistic.

—*Home Needlework* magazine
October 1899

Meticulous stitches add texture and pattern to their environment.

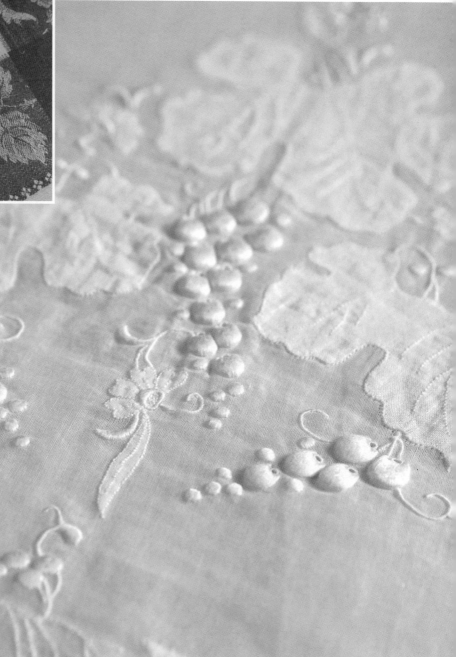

OPPOSITE: Table runner, circa 1940. Satin-stitch motifs and cutwork with needle-lace insertions and drawn-work borders.
ABOVE: Red-and-white fringed damask napkins with monogram.
RIGHT: Organza table runner, early twentieth century. Applied leaves and padded satin-stitched grapes. To achieve the dimensionality of the grapes, layers of vertically oriented satin stitch were worked atop horizontally oriented satin stitches.

Linens
TELL THE STORY OF A
Place

❦

Most linens speak to us with an accent. A quick glance through a dictionary of linens and laces sends the reader on a journey stretching across Europe and beyond. Even a woefully incomplete list is exhausting: Belgian lace, *broderie anglaise*, Dresden work, English lace, Egyptian lace, Greek lace, Indian lace, Irish lace, macramé (Moorish) lace, Madeira work, Milanese lace, Normandy lace, Russian lace, Scottish lace, Swiss embroidery, and Venetian needlepoint. Consider further those pieces of linen that speak not with a clearly defined accent, but in a *patois* or Creole: the pillows made in Paris by the daughter of Belgian lace makers; the tablecloth made in Vienna by the student of an Italian teacher; the bedspread made in an American colony by the daughter of English merchants. Labeling and attribution is not always an easy task.

Linens, and the embroidery techniques used to create them, are as much a story of rippling influences across lands and cultures as they are of the urge to decorate and beautify.

Pillow sham, Austria-Hungary, late-nineteenth century. The satin stitches that create this floral design are exquisite in their precision and were certainly rendered by an expert hand.

OPPOSITE PAGE: Filet net with crochet floral border and tassels. French, early twentieth century. RIGHT: Tablecloth with blue chain-stitched border, early twentieth century. BELOW: Crochet table covering with tatting and buttonhole stitch. Austria-Hungary, late nineteenth century.

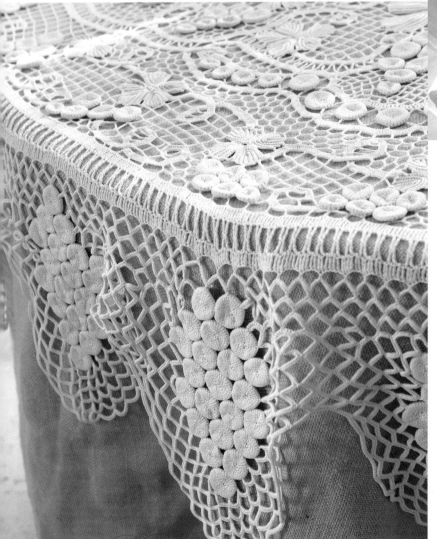

Techniques used to create the dazzling curtain panel hanging in the window of a seventeenth-century French *palais* can be traced backwards in time across trade routes and continental divides, into civilizations long gone. Every innovation bears the imprint of that which came before it; nothing is fixed in time. Studied intently enough, the method with which the twenty-first century needleworker employs a needle and thread to monogram a simple hand towel will send the studious observer leap-frogging into the past and landing upon the doorstep of the Garden of Eden, when Adam and Eve sewed fig leaves together and set in motion a desire to adorn and decorate that continues unabated today.

Little clues point to the corner of the world where

a piece of embroidery was created

Tablecloth with crochet edging bearing
Latin-cross motifs, early twentieth century.

CLOCKWISE: Two pillows with blue cross stitches, Greece or Southeast Europe, early twentieth century; Filet-lace antimacassar with bullion-loop trim, Italian, early twentieth century; Detail of bobbin-lace trim, Belgian, late-nineteenth century.

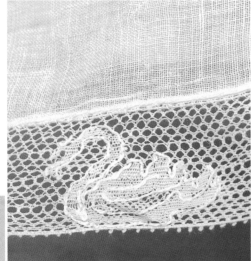

Sheer fabric adorned and festooned with *lace and ruffles* speak of Old World elegance and *lavish lifestyles.*

OPPOSITE PAGE: Sheer voile curtain with applied tape lace, cutwork, and filet-lace insertions. LEFT: Detail of filet-lace insertion. ABOVE: Sheer voile curtains with handmade filet-lace insertions, Austrian, circa 1860.

OPPOSITE PAGE: A variety of ecru pillows with crochet and bobbin-lace embellishments; and, in foreground, a cross-stitch sampler, circa 1907. RIGHT and BELOW: Lively pillow tops with red and blue embroidery speak of South-eastern European provenance.

pandora de balthazar
• A COLLECTOR'S PORTRAIT •

"Just come to Pensacola," Pandora de Balthazar says into the phone, "and I will show you linens that will make you weep."

When it comes to her vast collection of antique linens, Pandora isn't modest. A seasoned world traveler who has spent a decade and a half luring linens of staggering beauty out from Europe's secret hiding places, Pandora knows full well that when she gets you into her shop (aptly named Antique European Linens) in downtown Pensacola, Florida, she's going to take your breath away. She's used to dazzling people. Her greatest charm, however, is her boundless enthusiasm. When speaking about her antique textile collection—of which household linens make up a substantial portion—she is a cheerleader, professor, and dutiful foster mother all rolled into one.

Pandora can't remember a time when linens were not an important part of her life, when she did not enjoy the touch and texture of linens. As a child growing up in Dalton, Georgia, she loved to look through windows covered with lace curtains. Her mother, an accomplished seamstress and the first female manager for the Singer Sewing Company, instilled in Pandora a preference for quality over quantity: "She believed that if you could only afford to have one dress, then it was going to be a darn good one." As a young woman, Pandora discovered her gift for understanding numbers and gradually forged a career in corporate financial planning, through which she was able to travel the world and indulge her hobby for collecting antique linens.

While Pandora can't remember when textiles weren't a part of her life, she can, however, pinpoint the exact moment that they became the center of her life: 1996, when Hurricane Opal devastated Pensacola and washed her home, her office, and her

OPPOSITE PAGE: Three sets of trousseau pillow shams featuring a variety of fine techniques: scalloped and embroidered edges; hand-ruffled batiste edged in fine bobbin lace; and needle-lace edging and tucked needle-lace inserts . Bedside table features a needle-lace tablecloth. ABOVE and LEFT: Italian shadow embroidery on net, tucked and fringed with center of heavy bobbin lace, circa 1840. LEFT: Detail of curtain panel.

A sea of *white lace* evokes the image of *nimble fingers dancing* with white silks and flaxen threads.

beloved collection of linens out into the sea. But, as the saying goes, what doesn't kill you makes you stronger. With a small portion of her collection that was in a Texas storage facility at the time of the hurricane, she transitioned from antique linens collector to a dealer and, without a home to return to, she began criss-crossing the country in a van, traveling from antique show to antique show. A decade later, her business is firmly entrenched in downtown Pensacola and her clients come to her.

This account, however, leaves out the most exotic part of Pandora's story, the part that explains why she would leave behind a successful career in financial planning and devote herself to what had previously been a hobby; it is a story that she recounts with hushed reverence. While on vacation in Budapest, Hungary, in 1989, she met and subsequently married a Hungarian native, with whom she set up housekeeping in a 200-year old house in a tiny Hungarian village. She could be in Austria in an hour and in Italy in four, and she took full advantage of their proximity to supplement both her textiles collection and her expertise. Her neighbors back in Hungary, however, were adjusting to the post-Communist economy and, in search of hard dollars, began bringing Pandora their own family linens. "I became known as 'that American' who would buy and give them a fair price on textiles. I couldn't resist them," she

THIS PAGE: An assemblage of the finest embroidery from primitive to professional, boasting the finest needle-, bobbin-, and crochet-lace embellishments.

THIS PAGE: French-net curtain panels, linen appliqué
with tambour stitching. French, late nineteenth century.

recalls. "People wanted new things that they'd never seen before, things that the rest of the world had but they didn't. So they sold off the things that were old. The young people didn't want those antique things."

The pieces that began streaming into Pandora's collection were unlike anything she'd seen before: linen souvenirs of the mighty Austro-Hungarian Empire, a longstanding cultural and political powerhouse that had collapsed during the First World War, plus charming folk pieces that contained centuries of tradition within their elaborate stitches. Pandora was mesmerized and transformed. She bought all that she could, amassing a tremendous collection that she sent back to her family in the States for safekeeping. Pandora returned to Pensacola in 1995. Stripped of her home and her possessions a year later; she threw all of her energy into pursuing a new mission for which her entire life had prepared her.

Thus is the short account of how a girl from Dalton, Georgia, became a cheerleader, professor, and foster mother for antique linens created centuries ago on the opposite side of the globe. Each role is distinct. She is a cheerleader in that she genuinely loves and celebrates the cultures that still savor their linens, citing one of her favorite cities, Taormina, Sicily, as an example. "I adore how people put lace in all of their windows and don't think it's fussy," Pandora says. "Men expect a tablecloth and well-laid table. I adore where masculinity exists in an area we think is feminine." She'd like to see some of this Old-World sensibility transplanted in modern-day America.

In her professor role, Pandora is vigilant about educating people on the artistic and cultural value of antique linens in an effort to elevate the decorative arts to the level of fine arts. In this role, she seeks to save and preserve. The Ameri-

can public has been taught to find bargains, she says, but not to invest. "Textiles of old were made to be a family tradition, not made to be extinct within a few years," she says. "Today we lead a life that is a little more disposable. If you buy things at 'low-price store,' you're not attached to it; so what if you throw it away? But if you made it, or if you paid several thousand dollarsfor it, you're going to value it. In the past, people were raised by their families to appreciate their textiles."

And finally, Pandora is like a foster mother to the pieces in her collection, protecting them like endangered wildlife until she can find them a home in which she believes they will be treated and preserved in the way they deserve. No longer does she have to seek out linens from behind the closed doors and private collections of Europe; these days her textiles seem to find their way to her doorstep because their parting owners know that they are turning pieces of their family's history over to a compassionate caregiver. This reputation is one that has earned her a swelling roster of repeat clients, including a good number of Europeans who travel to Pensacola to purchase the cultural heirlooms that their parents' generation considered passé and foolishly sold away. When Pandora is confident that she has located a deserving family for a piece of her precious linen, she will open a window and allow it to fly away home. ▧

> *"Textiles of old were made to be a family tradition, not made to be extinct within a few years…people were raised by their families to appreciate their textiles."*

LEFT: Needle-lace trousseau pillow sham with very fine tucks, late nineteenth century. BELOW: Breakfast pillow (to be set in lap) with bobbin-lace insertions and edging and red satin-stitch coat-of-arms, French, nineteenth century. NEXT PAGE: Detail of a needle-lace tablecloth with cherubs, Italian, late nineteenth century.

ABOVE: Red-and-white woven cloth embellished with simple white embroidery stitches and needle-weaving and edged with bobbin-lace trim, late nineteenth century.

A Luncheon Set
WITH ALL THE CHARM
OF OLD WORLD STITCHERY

BY ETHELYN M. GUPPY

It is, of course, the most natural thing in the world that the great interest directed toward Central Europe at the present time, should be reflected in nearly every phase of decorative work, which the majority of us find so engaging—in our arts and crafts, embroideries and ornaments. There is another consideration, however, even more appealing to the woman who enjoys lovely, distinctive things for her home, yet who is practically a novice in the art of ornamental stitchery. As is well known, the peasant women in those lands across the sea which have been brought so near to us achieve the most wonderful results by the use of two or three simple stitches— rarely more in any single piece or design; and there is no form of embroidery more satisfactory and lasting in charm than that which is developed by these same women for their own use, and from their own inner inspiration. In the humblest homes are often found embroidered linens that would delight milady of the mansion, and do credit to her environment; and surely it affords calls for congratulation that these lovely things are easily within reach of the homemaking, housekeeping woman of our own country, who understands ordinary sewing and is willing to bring to her work the care and painstaking, which always assure success.

—*Needlecraft* Magazine
September 1927

OPPOSITE: Dining-room chair slipcovers fashioned from monogrammed antique damask hand towels (circa 1900), sheer voile, and a hand-loomed tablecloth with crochet edging dating to the Austro-Hungarian Empire period. Slipcovers are an innovative way to enjoy antique draperies and tablecloths whose proportions do not lend themselves to use with contemporary furniture.

• A MOMENT IN THE SUN •

Pandora de Balthazar encourages her clients to think creatively when displaying their linens. In the picture above, Pandora used a tablecloth with exquisite filet-lace panels to dress a window for a special occasion. For the valance, she used an ecru banquet tablecloth made of Venetian tape lace. The photo at left shows a detail of the Venetian tape-lace tablecloth: a marvel in which thousands of tiny, airy stitches provide support and stability to the meandering tape-lace patterns.

Linens
TELL A STORY OF
Home

Home, and home beautifying, is an art form that women have taken seriously for generations. A nineteenth-century interior decoration manual, *Dainty Work for Pleasure and Profit*, carried an exhortation for its gentle readers:

> *It is certainly the first duty of a wife and mother to make home the pleasantest and happiest spot on earth for the members of her family, and to do this requires more than order, system, immaculate cleanliness, more than the purchase of expensive carpets and heavy furniture. It requires the home-making, home-beautifying talent. It needs the exercise of an ingenious mind and nimble fingers in fashioning dainty accessories…and the numberless odds and ends that go to make up the pretty home comfort of a room.*

And therein lies the charm of the antique and vintage textiles. Though they conformed to requirements of necessity and function, and although they reflected artistic trends and decorating sensibilities of the day, they are still, in the end, a souvenir of (most often) a solitary woman's artistic process. In our present day, when the most delightful linens are to be had by a mere trip to the store or visit to a catalog Web site, we neglect to stretch

LEFT and BELOW: A linen tablecloth with delicate machine-embroidered flowers on sheer voile, circa 1920, has been refashioned by Pandora de Balthazar into a large pillow sham. The matching napkins bear the monogram of the original owner. OPPOSITE: Simple cross-stitched floral motif add a burst of color to a set of hemstitched linen napkins.

our own artistic muscles and talents, talents that many of our foremothers honed at a young age. How exciting it is to hold in our hands a piece of linen stitched long ago, and search for the personality of the woman who made it, to imagine her home, to feel the sincerity with which she poured her talent into a simple "home beautifying" project. We all long for our homes, the comfortable place where we can set aside our worries, relax, and be ourselves. Our homes are invaluable. From this perspective, these linen artifacts of homes from another time are more priceless than diamonds and rubies and contain all the blessings of heaven within them.

LEFT: The blue thread used in this tea towel indicates that it was created as part of a trousseau set. BELOW: Two hand towels embellished with drawn-thread patterns and punch work. The removal of threads weakens the fabric, so decorative stitches are added to provide added support as well as visual interest.

Tea towels and tablecloths of generations past find new expression in **homes of today.**

OPPOSITE PAGE: Tablecloths from two trousseau sets demonstrate differences in style: the monograms of the *AP* set are smaller and more elaborate, while the *O'N* cloth displays extravagantly padded satin-stitch letters. Toward the end of the nineteenth century in England there was a reaction against flowery embroidery and a preference for clear, plain letters in embroidery.

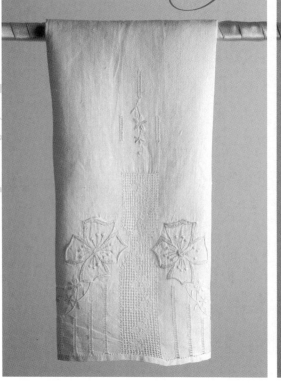

RIGHT: Kimeran Stevens personalized this simple vintage damask hand towel with tatted edging by adding her own machine-embroidered monogram. BELOW: Layers of sheer fabric work together to form a pretty bow in this vintage pink-and-white fingertip towel.

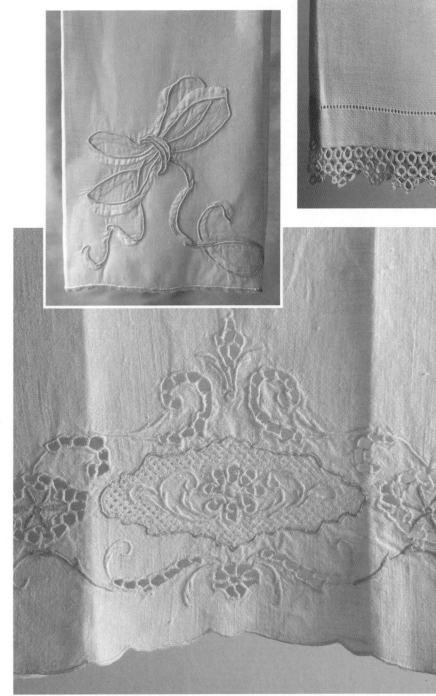

LEFT and OPPOSITE PAGE: Although the workmanship of these vintage hand towels is less-than-expert, the patient effort with which they were created still speak of beautifully decorated homes in decades past. Because hand towels were an indispensable item in any home, the addition of embroidery by the women of the home lent an air of refined civility in even the most humble of circumstances.

RIGHT: The cutwork, drawn work, and sat-in stitches of these simple Hardanger-style napkins have firmly stood the test of time. OPPOSITE PAGE: Mix-and-match vintage hand towels form new families from separated sets.

kimeran stevens

• A COLLECTOR'S PORTRAIT •

Kimeran Stevens is a homemaker in the most genuine sense of the word. She has devoted most of her adult life to making her home the happiest, most pleasant spot on earth for her husband and two sons. But it's a pretty happy place for the friends who visit, too. Whenever she hosts a dinner party or luncheon, Kimeran almost always goes to a lot of trouble to create a special dining environment for her guests: starched tablecloths, fabric napkins, elegant placemats, and creative centerpieces. The intention behind her effort is not to demonstrate what a skilled hostess she is, though; her intention is to make every guest feel valuable. Swaddling them in custom-pressed fabric is just one of her secret ways of giving her guests an extra hug.

"I want you to feel like you were loved and cherished when you came into my home," Kimeran says. She and her husband, Bill, host frequent dinner parties for their Sunday-school class of newly married or engaged couples, and many of the couples are new to town, new to their church, and in search of a community of friends. The dinner parties are designed to get everyone together outside of church and put couples at ease with the upheaval in their lives. In Kimeran's opinion, the little details like fancy napkins make a big difference: "It says, 'I like you. I love you. I cherish you.' It makes the kids think, 'they went to a lot of trouble for me,' and that makes them feel valuable."

Kimeran is proof that you don't have to grow up with a tablecloth on the table for every meal to appreciate the subtle luxury that linens add to a home environment. Her own mother set

THIS PAGE: Tablecloth with cutwork and sat-in-stitch floral motifs, drawn-thread borders, and machine-made fig-ural lace insertion, circa 1940. Reminiscent of Appenzell-style embroi-dery, this lace insertion was likely sold on a pa-per card.

her table without a linen covering, but the dinner table nevertheless was an anchor and gathering place for her family. "Mom was a good cook, and we sat down to dinner every night." Kimeran continued the tradition of sitdown meals with her own family, but as she got older she began to supplement the ritual with a growing collection of linens.

"I've always liked to set a pretty table, but I didn't have any fine linen until I was in my thirties and forties" she explains. But she's always enjoyed working with her hands, and was already accustomed to putting her hand into service for home-beautifying projects. ("We didn't have anything to go on our walls when we first got married, so I made things like that to go on them," she says, pointing to a cross-stitched sampler hanging in her kitchen.) When their boys were in middle school, Kimeran and Bill joined a supper club, and that's when the bug for creating beautiful tablescapes and personalized home linens really struck.

"I call it my 'frou-frou,'" Kimeran says of her carefully laid tables she creates for her friends. That description, however, isn't entirely correct. The dictionary defines "frou-frou" as "fussy or showy ornamentation," and popular usage implies silly ostentation. While Kimeran certainly fusses over her tables, it is for a noble cause: to convey thought and purpose in a day and age when most of us are rushed and looking for shortcuts. For a recent going away luncheon for a neighbor from Pakistan, to which all their neighbors were invited, Kimeran set a very traditional white-on-white table. "I think everyone was impressed that I bothered," she says. "But I wanted [the neighbor] to leave the South with a good flavor in her mouth and to show her, 'You'll never be loved anywhere else on earth as much as you were loved here.'"

Plus, much of the personalization and ornamentation of her linens is a labor of love that Kimeran performs herself. The top-of-the-line machine she has in her sewing room is considerably fancier than her first sewing machine—which she bought with money she received as gifts upon graduation from college—but she loves it to death. "I can't do handwork anymore because my wrists and hands hurt. The machine embroidery is so much faster and it gives me instant gratification," she says. She uses her machine to bring a warm flavor of home to friends new and old who pass through her life. "Most of my work I give away. I've monogrammed countless wedding, baby, housewarming, and hostess gifts," she says.

Her "frou-frou" collection is rounded out with a good number of vintage items. "I didn't inherit any fine linen from my family, so most of my vintage pieces I've collected at markets and estate sales. I feel victorious when I buy stained linens and am able to get the stain out," she says. Although these pieces didn't come from her own family, she still loves to use them and imagine their use in someone else's home long ago. "I like the personal side of history. When we visited Mount Vernon, I was more interested in the bedspreads than what they had on their shelves," she says.

"None of these pieces from my family are valuable, but I feel more connected to have something that they held, touched, and handled in their personal lives."

Linens need not be elaborately embroidered to bring

sparkle to a room.

LEFT: Tablerunner with colorful embroidery, circa 1950. BELOW: Scalloped-edge napkins with simple cutwork floral motifs. OPPOSITE PAGE: Vintage laundry bag embellished with padded satin stitch, stem stitch, and French knots.

Tucked into drawers in her extra bedroom, Kimeran does have a number of small pieces—doilies, coasters, bread cloths—that belonged to her grandparents, and she treasures them as much as she treasures the glorious linens that are the signature mark of her fancy dinner parties. "None of these pieces from my family are valuable, but I feel more connected to have something that they held, touched, and handled in their personal lives. It makes me feel close to them," she says. This closeness and this connection conveyed by the fibers of soft cloth is the same sentiment that she seeks to extend to her new family: the friends and neighbors that she graciously welcomes into her home. ▩

LEFT: King-sized trousseau sheet with hand-applied ruffles and matching male and female pillows. Large openings inside the drawn-work border of sheet allowed ribbons to be changed with the seasons. Austrian pillow shams bear heavily embroidered roses in "trousseau blue" thread. Silk bedcover boasts intricate Milanese needle-lace insertions. French pointe d'esprit lace drapes form a canopy for the bed. BELOW: A bolster pillow was fashioned from a French hand-applied Normandy-lace bedcover.

LEFT and BELOW (detail): A tear down the center of a banquet-sized, Madeira-embroidery tablecloth rendered it unusable for its original purpose. Repurposed as drapery accents and a lambrequin, the damaged tablecloth has taken on new life.

When it comes to decorating with a piece of linen, you must treat it *like a work of art*

Gifts for the
HOUSEKEEPER

BY ANGELA H. BARRETT

There is no housekeeper but has room for "just one more" doily or centerpiece, and when we hesitate over what to get such a friend we may be assured that one of these useful and pretty bits of household fitting will be just the thing. Nor need we, when time is pressing, and there are so many gifts to make ready, spend too much care and work upon them. It is really marvelous to note the charming effects produced by the simplest stitch nowadays. Take, as an example, that known of old as feather stitch, perhaps more correctly designated coral or briarstitch. Of this, as of most others, the buttonholed stitch is the foundation. Draw the thread up through the material, turning it in a loop to the right, and hold it down with the left thumb. Insert the needle about 1/8" from the place where the thread was drawn through, take a stitch of the same length, slanting downward from right to left, draw through, and repeat on the other side, reversing the process-that is, turning the thread to the left and slanting the stitch from left to right. Having learned to make the plain or single stitch, it may be varied almost indefinitely; and a little practice will give the "knack" of doing it quickly and evenly.

—*Needlecraft* magazine
October 1913

• *Folk* •
NEELDLEWORK

This bright blue thread used to embellish this small, round table cloth points to Eastern European provenance. Rich blues, reds, and golds embellished the folk needlework of this area, in stark contrast to the white-on-white embroidery that dominated in Western Europe.

*W*hether *simple or elaborate,* every piece of linen deserves to be valued on its own.

RIGHT: Three doilies with crochet edging. Example in foreground created from "punch work"-style embroidery. OPPOSITE PAGE: Detail of a cutwork linen bed cover, Austro-Hungarian Empire period.

Linens
TELL A STORY OF
Tradition

Tradition. It is the backbone of a body of work—that of embroidered linens—which began in ancient times and continues in our homes today. Browse the Old Masters section of your favorite museum and notice how often tablecloths and hand linens bearing flourishes of embroidery and lace are depicted in the paintings. Step into the gallery of Medieval painting and notice the omnipresence of linens swaddling Mary and the infant Jesus and of linens covering the Lord's Table. It would seem that every milestone in history has been accompanied by a piece of linen covered in exquisite handwork.

Most of us, however, don't have to visit a museum to realize that our love of linens is rooted in tradition. We have only to look at the tablecloth that once graced our grandmother's dinner table, or admire the tidy monogram in the corner of the handkerchief that was once tucked into our grandfather's jacket pocket. A

Pillow sham, Austrian, circa 1900. Intricate cutwork floral motifs joined by wrapped bars; scalloped cutwork trim. Filet-lace curtain panel in background.

bride-to-be registering for linens in a fancy department store today is in many ways building her wedding trousseau, a tradition practiced for generation upon generation in many different parts of the world. We have only to open our eyes to notice how often linens are present at the important moments of our lives. And if we are to take a cue from the past, we should lavish these ubiquitous linens with all the affection and care that we would offer a faithful companion.

OPPOSITE: Crib pillow, American early twentieth century. Contains a unique mélange of hand-made laces, including Irish crochet, and applied machine-made laces. Left: Linen table cloth, circa 1920. Cross-stitched rose motifs and crocheted trim.

Napkins, early twentieth century. Drawn work medallion surrounded by cutwork floral motifs and satin-stitch monogram. For centuries, inventories of wealthy families listed items such as napkins and tablecloths by the dozens. Inventories of the emerging nineteenth-century middle class, however, often listed these items in multiples of three and six.

-Unusual-
TABLE SETS

Within the last few years, we have been gradually breaking away from the idea that all dining room tables must be arranged alike in snowy white damask. Especially for informal meals, less formal table appointments are permissible. Pleasure may be added to the daily meals when the housewife is the fortunate possessor of a variety of pretty luncheon sets. With the most inexpensive materials any woman who is at all able to handle a needle can obtain decidedly gratifying results.

A table runner and place mat might be in unbleached muslin, cretonne and rick rack braid, furnishing ample evidence for this assertion. A commendable feature with this type of work is that one can place the flower motifs wherever one may choose to have them. Another delightfully simple but pleasing model is the fringed doily. Old blue ratine has been used for a set consisting of a centerpiece, plate, and tumbler doilies.

To make a centerpiece 18 inches in diameter, draw a circle measuring 16 inches, then draw another line two inches outside of this circle. This will be the cutting line, the fringe being two inches wide.

—*The Modern Priscilla*
May 1922

ABOVE: Round tablecloth, French, circa 1860. Combination of bobbin lace and needle lace; the fleur de lis medallions were pre-made and sold on cards. Inventive needleworkers could incorporate these time-saving insertions into their own handwork for dramatic effects. RIGHT: Detail of a needle-lace insertion on a tablecloth, worked primarily in detached buttonhole stitch. The main shapes of the needle lace were worked on a separate surface—usually parchment—and then joined together within the cutwork panel.

Distinctive motifs and techniques travel the century, passed down from mother to daughter, and from master to apprentice.

Without the distraction of color,
white embroidery on white linen allows *expertly executed stitches* to take center stage.
The result is a veritable *feast for the eye.*

martha pullen
• A COLLECTOR'S PORTRAIT •

The tradition of linens, for Martha Pullen, began on the dining room table where her grandmother served her famous fried chicken and homemade biscuits. Her grandmother was a school teacher in a one-room school house in Scottsboro, Alabama, and her husband, Martha's grandfather, was a farmer and carpenter. Their household linens were not the stuff of royalty, but what they did have shaped the world and the habits of young Martha Pullen.

"My grandmother had no fine linens but she loved her damask tablecloths and one was always on her dining room table when anyone came to visit. She also loved linen napkins and her plain ones were always at the table," Martha recalls. The tradition continued with the next generation, Martha's mother: "On all special occasions Mama would cover our dining room table with one of her prized tablecloths and

place her prettiest cloth napkins at each place setting along with her sterling silver, best china, and crystal."

The first gift of Martha's married life was a hand-embroidered tablecloth made lovingly for Martha and her new husband, Joe, by Martha's mother. "Mama wanted to make a cross stitched tablecloth for my sister and for me. She purchased two kits of ecru fabric with the stitches stamped on the fabric. Her floss was medium tan," Martha says. "Every time I would visit with Mama and Daddy in their home she would be stitching on the tablecloths. There was such love going into that massive amount

LEFT: Infant's pillow, circa 1940. Floral motifs created using satin stitch and stem stitch; "baby" executed with double back-stitch, a stitch that creates heavy thread coverage on reverse side of work, almost simulating shadow work when worked on light-weight sheer fabrics. THIS PAGE: Bridge-cover tablecloth, circa 1940. Appenzell work, satin and seed stitches, and drawn work.

of cross stitch that I knew would last longer than either the maker or the receiver."

Martha was lucky enough to marry into a linen-loving family, as well. "I truly use tablecloths inherited from both my family and from Joe's family," she says. "I use bridge cloths on my card tables to seat four people for dinner. Joe's mother loved to play bridge and always had her card tables set beautifully with refreshments as her Tuesday and Wednesday clubs arrived. Her cloths and napkins matched and usually had wonderful colored hand embroidery."

"With today's modern sewing machines, monograms can be accomplished in a very short time with beautiful plain purchased napkins or tablecloths that just scream for embroidery."

Martha's fascination with vintage clothing is well know by her audience of heirloom sewing enthusiasts, so they probably wouldn't be surprised to learn that she's indulged her love of household linens during her trips around the world. "On my first trip to Paris I remember so well purchasing small cocktail napkins with various birds printed on them. I think I purchased about 100 of these small napkins to use at large parties that we sometimes give," she says. "On my first trip to Switzerland, I purchased tablecloths with angels embroidered in gold on the Swiss embroidery. Christmas was coming and I love Christmas linens! I always tried to purchase these beautiful linens for my mother and for Joe's mother when we traveled because I knew table linens or napkins of any kind would be their favorite souvenir from our travels."

The souvenirs of Martha's travels are practical: she purchases a tablecloth and matching napkins from each country she visits. "My guess would be that from my purchased collection to my inherited collection, I have a little bit of everything from crocheted doilies to European tablecloths adorned with hand embroidery and lace to kitchen printed cloths with everything from flowers to cherries to souvenir maps printed on them," Martha says. One of her most special items, however, is a "gorgeous" French-lace tablecloth given to her by Dr. Elizabeth Rhodes, Dean of the Fashion School at Kent State University.

Martha has successfully passed the love of linens down to the next generation, and crossed the gender divide, as well. "I have both white and ecru purchased napkins with the letter *P* monogrammed on them. For our dentist son's fortieth birthday, I asked him what did he want that would be very special and he answered, 'I want twelve white napkins embroidered with the same *P* that you have on your napkins.' That is exactly what he got and he loved them," Martha says, with a note of pride in her voice. "I actually did fourteen for him since napkins have a way of somehow getting stained or lost occasionally. With today's modern sewing machines, monograms can be accomplished in a very short time with beautiful plain purchased napkins or tablecloths that just scream for embroidery."

Martha has a cautionary tale for lovers of linens who are just beginning the process of collecting vintage and antique pieces. "Many years ago when visiting in Lunn's Antiques in London, the owner, Stephen, told me, 'Martha, since I know you love embroidery I am going to show you one of the most beautiful tablecloths that I have ever come across.' He left the front room of the shop shortly to return with a small white circular tablecloth with the name

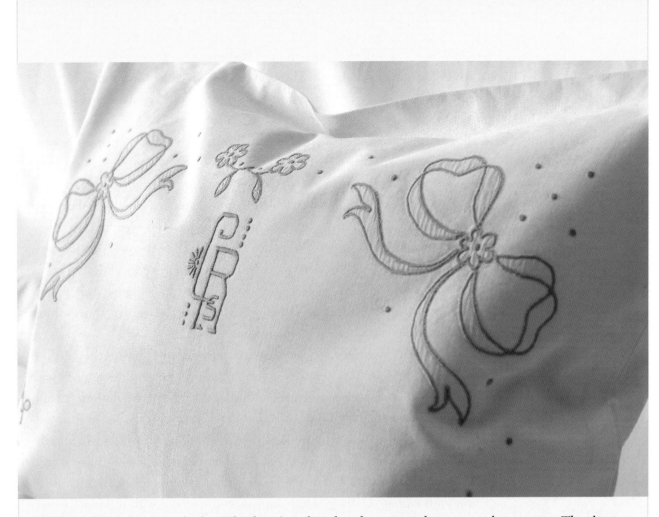

PREVIOUS PAGE: Trousseau bed sheet and pillow sham, late nineteenth century. Appenzell work, satin stitch, and cutwork. ABOVE: Pillowcase, early- to mid-twentieth century. Satin stitch monogram with art-nouveau influence; appliqué bows and flowers. NEXT PAGE: Three pillows, twentieth century. Left: Cutwork with needle-lace insertions and filet-lace trim. Center: Drawn work with dove's eye motifs and drawn-work border on ruffle. Right: Netting with machine embroidery.

'Charlotte' embroidered exquisitely across the center. The letters were reasonably large and probably stretched about twenty inches across the top-center of the cloth. Other beautiful embroidery was scalloped around the outside edges; however, the word, 'Charlotte' was definitely the focal point," Martha recalls. "Frankly the tablecloth was very expensive and, although I was passionately drawn to it, I decided not to spend the money since my plan for that trip was to purchase christening dresses." Martha says she has spent the past 25 years regretting not purchasing the cloth.

"I learned a very important lesson. When an antique piece 'speaks' to me, if I can possibly afford the purchase, then I ought to 'not purchase' something else (or several 'something elses') so I can take home the item that touches my heart the way the 'Charlotte' tablecloth did." Your passion for a piece that touches your heart, Martha says, will be evident to everyone who comes in contact with it. Who knows? Maybe a little girl eating fried chicken and biscuits around a table set with your prized tablecloth might be inspired to make antique fabric creations the center of her professional life, as well. It has happened before. ▓

~New Luncheon Linens~
MATCHING ULTRA
SIMPLICITY WITH SMARTNESS

BY HELEN GRANT

S traight from Paris, they come to us, these fascinating little linens, and they reflect the new Parisian spirit, which is finding expression and all manner of household and personal accoutrements. That the vogue of simplicity has captured that famous fashion center, as well as "the Paris of America" and the world in general, there is little question; and this seems particularly true in the needleworking realm. The demand for simple designs, so easily and quickly developed in equally simple and familiar embroidery stitches that the doing is a joy to the busiest of home women, is insistent and permits no deviation from its edict; at the same time, there is always the proviso that artistic effect be not sacrificed to ease and rapidity of execution.

—*Needlecraft* magazine
January 1927

Linens
TELL A STORY OF
Family

———— ❦ ————

They are singular works of art. Stark and bold or delicate and lacey, the meticulously designed lines of a monogram carry within them the weight of history, the pride of ownership, the representation of family, and a designation of social status. They are at once infinitely simple and complex.

When we take a closer look at monograms, despite their myriad styles and letter combinations, time slows down and almost stops. The letters that compose our monograms in the early twenty-first century are rooted in the early Phoenician letterforms dating to 1500 B.C. For centuries when the capability to write was confined to an elite, educated few, artists marked their works with a monogram that served as a signature. Prosperous families of the Middle Ages used monograms to identify everything from their houses to their possessions. When worked on linen, a much more malleable medium than wood, metal, or stone, the monogram quickly evolved into an art form of staggering beauty.

Those of us today who are without a drop of noble blood probably do not appreciate the fringe benefits of living in a democratic society in which we are free to embroider our initials on anything we please. In fourteenth-century England, a law was decreed that forbade anybody below a certain income level to wear embroidered costumes; the use of monograms by those of the middling and lower stations in life was similarly verboten. Not until the end of the sixteenth century did the use of monograms gain acceptance for members of the general public.

Just as embroidered linens were symbolic of wealth and nobility, so too were the monograms placed upon these pieces; to convey the message of wealth, linens needed to be displayed to guests. Monograms were meant to be seen, and visibility encouraged innovation. Linen cupboards and armoires were developed to display easily stacks upon stacks of neatly monogrammed items. In the nineteenth century, when elaborate centerpieces on tables became fashionable, monograms on large tablecloths

were often moved from the center point of the table; instead, two sets of monograms were offset to either side of the center position lest they be obscured. When the notion of social mobility evolved alongside organized industry in nineteenth-century Europe, the symbolism of monograms became exaggerated and re-energized by the aspirations of an ascendant middle class.

When we untangle the history of the letters used to create monograms we also gain an appreciation of the quirks and evolution of the English language. The letter *J*, for example, is nowhere to be found among monograms of Medieval times because it did not yet exist in the written language. *J* was still considered the consonant form of the letter *I*, so the handkerchief of a man named James King would have been marked with the initials *IK*. Similarly, *U* and *V* were considered to be vowel and consonant forms of the same letter; two instances of the letter *V* were eventually fused together to become the letter *W*. When trying to determine

• INNOVATION IN MONOGRAMMING •

For centuries, embroidery patterns were transferred to fabric via a method called "pouncing": a needleworker would dust a fine powder, such as pulverized charcoal, over a design pricked out of a piece of vellum placed atop her needlework fabric. The innovation of copper dye-cut stencils in the nineteenth century, such as these by the German manufacturer Künstler, made the process easier, quicker, and more affordable. Monograms could be brushed onto fabric with ink using the simpler tools shown here.

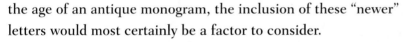

the age of an antique monogram, the inclusion of these "newer" letters would most certainly be a factor to consider.

Besides making monograms socially accessible to a wider audience, industrialization also revolutionized the ease with which monograms could be executed on all manner of linens. Pre-embroidered, raised satin stitch monograms were invented that could be sewn directly to linens using matching thread. Die-cut metal templates bearing monograms in a variety of styles and sizes enabled homemakers to imitate the elaborate stylings of professional needleworkers who, for centuries, were in the exclusive employ of royalty and the noble classes.

Even today, monograms continue to enchant and delight us with both their practicality and their artistry. Highly adaptable to the fashion of the day, the monogram has not yet encountered an environment that renders it obsolete. If anything, monograms prove the truism that "the more things change, the more they stay the same." In our world today, in which we are inundated with marketing messages and images at every turn, it is comforting to realize that the hand- and machine-stitched monograms that we so admire began as personal logos that have changed only negligibly over hundreds of years.

OPPOSITE and ABOVE:
Two monograms, meticulously executed in padded satin stitch and seed stitches on fine damask fabrics. Until the nineteenth century, white damask was the only linen used in the dining rooms of the well-to-do. But just as mechanical innovations made the art of monogramming more accessible to a broader audience, the invention of the Jacquard loom in 1805 brought damask fabrics to a wider audience as well. The automated production of damask and the increasing substitution of cotton for linen meant that damask napkins and tablecloths were for the first time accessible to more than just society's elite.

*M*onograms are at once infinitely *simple and* **complex**

-*The New Markings*-
FOR FINE LINENS

BY SONJA DANFELDT

The correct and artistic marking of the household linens is an all important and pleasant problem, which faces the bride-to-be, as well as the experienced housewife. There are no hard and fast rules as to the style or size of the monograms…other women who enjoy a variety would use one style for table linen, another for bed linen, another for personal use.

Some general rules for placing monograms on linens may be helpful. Sheets have the letters in the middle of the top about an inch from the hem or two inches from a scallop edge. Turn base of letters towards the hem or scallop. Pillowcases have the letters placed just above the hems in the middle of the top side with the base toward the hem or scallop. The sizes of monograms for sheets are usually two to six inches, for pillowcases, two to four inches; for a bedspread, six to fourteen inches.

On a table cloth, the monograms should preferably be placed about two inches from the edge of the table facing the corner of the cloth. When two sets of monograms are used, the most effective position is on each side of the center, so placed as to be a proper distance from both centerpieces and plates, with the base of the letters towards the table edge. In marking an embroidered luncheon cloth, be guided by the design. Napkins are usually marked in the diagonal of one corner with the base of the letter toward the corner.

—*Modern Priscilla*
November 1921

ABOVE: Textured stitches worked upon a padded base give the lines of this monogram the appearance of rope. The skill level necessary to execute this stitch is indicative of a professional embroiderer.

ABOVE: The earl's coronet atop the floral monogram on this bobbin-lace trimmed handkerchief indicates it once belonged to a noble family. It is worked entirely in satin stitch, with several pulled eyelet stitch. LEFT: The laurel wreath has long been a popular motif for embroiderers. Executed in lightly padded satin stitch, this monogram adorns an early twentieth-century damask tablecloth.

The lines of a monogram
can convey wealth and prestige.

LEFT: The small orbs and elongated diamond shapes that embellish the nobleman's coronet atop this exquisite monogram represent the jewels that would have decorated an actual headpiece, to be worn in official ceremonies. RIGHT: A nobleman's coronet decorates the interlocking lines of a "G" and a "M." The damask fabric on which it is stitched is as fine a quality as the monogram itself. NEXT PAGE: Three handkerchiefs, embellished with padded satin stich.

A Vintage
DO-IT-YOURSELF KIT

While monograms were once the exclusive domain of the nobles classes, the dawning of the Industrial Age brought these distinctive family symbols to the emerging middle class. Anyone who could afford to buy a monogram stencil kit, such as this vintage example of German manufacture (right), could give her own linens a distinctive mark.

NEUHEIT!

E B

KREUZSTICH-SCHABLONEN

Modelos pour broderie du linge.
Modeli per ricamare la lingeria.
Metal-Stencils for Embroidering of Linen.

RIGHT: A stunning example, this three-letter monogram is worked in padded satin stitch with drawn-thread work defining the major lines of the letters. BELOW: Another exquisite monogram, worked in padded satin stitch and steed stitches. Monograms of this variety were often engraved into silver and other precious metals that families wanted to identify with their own distinct mark.

The beautiful, interlocking lines of a finely wrought monogram are enough to take one's breath away with *sheer delight*.

Initials & Monograms
PADDED SATIN STITCH

The Padded Satin Stitch is a type still used a great deal on bed linen. The thicker parts of each letter are first outlined with fine running or chain stitches and then padded with a bold running or chain stitch. Should a highly embossed letter be required a second layer of chain stitch is worked over the first and possibly a third line or two down the center. All padding stitches should follow the outline of the letter, working round and round within until the centre is reached. The covering satin stitches  are then added and to prevent puckering are better worked in an embroidery frame. Make each satin stitch slant…and cover the finer lines of the letters with closely worked stem stitching. Ordinary cro- chet cotton gives a firm solid padding for large letters with the satin stitch worked in a good quality linen thread.

—*Mary Thomas's Embroidery Book*, 1936
page 172

OPPOSITE PAGE: The three letters of this unusual monogram, *SZE*, are worked in padded satin stitch and outlined with black thread in running stitch. The tablecloth that the monogram embellishes is a stunning example of damask weave. LEFT: The scrolling lines of this two-letter monogram, *PB*, are so finely intertwined that the eye has to work to distinguish the letters. The monogram is worked in padded satin stitch with fuchsia thread and embellished with simple floral motifs.

Tiny • MONOGRAMS •

Less than 7/8" tall, this petite monogram—VM—sacrifices no complexity to compensate for its small size. Worked in padded satin stitch and stem stitch, the tiny stitches that create this monogram required the utmost skill and patience. The damask napkins that the monogram embellishes is pictured in entirety on page 43.

ACKNOWLEDGEMENTS

This book could not have been produced without the invaluable contributions of many people. In particular, I wish to extend a sincere and humble "thank you" to the following key contributors:

To **Martha Pullen,** publisher, teacher, and connoisseur *par excellence* of fine sewing, whose wisdom, enthusiasm, and innovative mind has brought the techniques of the past to an entirely new generation of needleworkers;

To **Phyllis Hoffman,** president of Hoffman Media, whose business acumen and creative vision not only made this book possible, but teaches us that the "feminine arts" are more relevant than ever in the busy lives we lead today;

To **Pandora de Balthazar** and **Martha Lauren,** who graciously shared their extensive linen collections with Hoffman Media and provided education and insight about the pieces that fill these pages; and to **Kimeran Stevens**, who shared her heart and her home with us;

To **Marcy Black,** photographer, who masterfully harnessed the intangible qualities of light and atmosphere to convey the most delicate nuances of texture and pattern in every piece of linen that she photographed;

To **Jordan Marxer,** art director, whose exquisite taste and insistence upon graphic perfection reflected the exacting standards with which master needleworkers once approached their own work;

To **Greg Baugh,** production director, whose precise scheduling and practical vision plucked the ideas and images of this book out of the misty ether of creative minds and rendered them in print for all to enjoy;

To **Delisa McDaniel,** color technician, who worked tirelessly to ensure that every image fulfilled the vision of everyone involved;

To **Karen Dauphin,** copy editor, whose enthusiasm for antique linens and insightful feedback on text and concepts provided valuable momentum for the book-writing process;

To **Lorna Reeves,** Hoffman Media Needlework Division Director, and **Christy Schmitz**, editorial assistant, whose invaluable assistance enabled the editor to immerse herself in the world of antique linens;

And most importantly, to the women and girls—all of them anonymous—who created the masterpieces contained in this book. If only they could know, as they spent hour upon hour occupied with needle and thread, that an audience bigger than they could ever imagine would one day find joy and inspiration in the work of their hands.

—ELIZABETH PUGH, EDITOR

CREDITS

We would like to express our heartfelt gratitude to the following businesses for their role in making this book a reality:

Antique European Linens/Pandora de Balthazar Timeless
9 South Ninth Avenue, Pensacola, Florida 32502
Telephone: 850-432-4777
and
201 East Austin Street, Round Top, Texas 78954
Telephone: 979-249-2070
Web site: *www.antiqueeuropeanlinens.com*
E-mail: *sales@antiqueeuropeanlinens.com*

Martha Lauren Antique Linens and Accessories
2417 Canterbury Road, Mountain Brook, Alabama 35223
Telephone: 205-871-2283

Interiors at Pepper Place
(photography location)
2817 Second Avenue South, Birmingham, Alabama 35233
Telephone: 205-323-2817

SELECTED BIBLIOGRAPHY

Clabburn, Pamela. *The Needleworker's Dictionary.* New York: William Morrow & Company, Inc., 1976.

De Bonneville, Francoise. *The Book of Fine Linen.* Paris: Flammarion, 1999.

De Dillmont, Thérèse. *The Complete Encyclopedia of Needlework.* Philadelphia: Running Press, 1978.

Earnshaw, Pat. *A Dictionary of Lace.* New York: Dover Publications, 1999.

Heron, Addie E. *Dainty Work for Pleasure and Profit.* Chicago: Thompson & Thomas, 1984.

Reigate, Emily. *An Illustrated Guide to Lace.* Suffolk, England: Antique Collectors' Club, Ltd., 1986.

Scofield, Elizabeth and Peggy Zalamea. *20th Century Linens and Lace: A Guide to Identification, Care, and Prices of Household Linens.* Algen, Pennsylvania: Schiffer Publishing Ltd., 1995.

Warnick, Kathleen and Shirley Nilsson. *Legacy of Lace: Identifying, Collecting, and Preserving American Lace.* New York: Crown Publishers, Inc. 1988.

EMBROIDERIES

The embroidery designs shown are a sampling of the many patterns featured on the linens. These may be enlarged for hand embroidery or are available for machine embroidery (all formats) on CD-ROM from Martha Pullen Company.

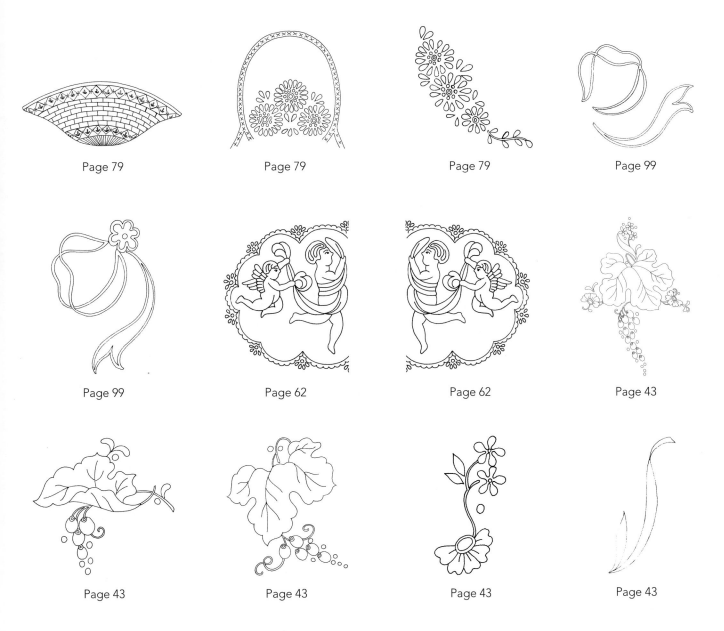

Page 79

Page 79

Page 79

Page 99

Page 99

Page 62

Page 62

Page 43

Page 43

Page 43

Page 43

Page 43

Page 71

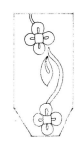

Page 71

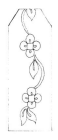

Page 71

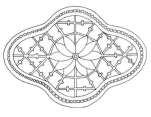

Page 24

Page 106

Page 72

Page 72

Page 72

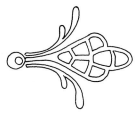

Page 72

Page 72

Page 72

Page 11

Page 13

Page 17

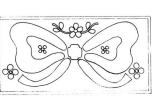

Page 71

Page 75

Page 42

Page 42

Page 42

Page 42

Page 95

Page 95

Page 95

Page 95

Page 67

Page 67

Page 74

Page 107

Page 28

Page 28

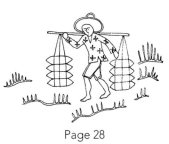

Page 28

Page 28

Page 79

Page 79

Page 79

Page 95

Page 95

Page 95

Page 95

Page 95

Page 95

Page 95

Page 95

Page 95

Page 77

Page 73

Page 73

Page 95

Page 71

Page 71

Page 13